Best Easy Bike Rides
Gettysburg

Help Us Keep This Guide Up to Date

Every effort has been made by the author and editors to make this guide as accurate and useful as possible. However, many things can change after a guide is published—trails are rerouted, regulations change, techniques evolve, facilities come under new management, etc.

We appreciate hearing from you concerning your experiences with this guide and how you feel it could be improved and kept up to date. While we may not be able to respond to all comments and suggestions, we'll take them to heart and we'll also make certain to share them with the author. Please send your comments and suggestions to the following address:

Globe Pequot Press
Reader Response/Editorial Department
246 Goose Lane, Suite 200
Guilford, CT 06437

Thanks for your input!

Best Easy Bike Rides Series

Best Easy Bike Rides Gettysburg

Tom Hammell

FALCONGUIDES

GUILFORD, CONNECTICUT

FALCONGUIDES®

An imprint of The Rowman & Littlefield Publishing Group, Inc.
4501 Forbes Blvd., Ste. 200
Lanham, MD 20706
www.rowman.com
Falcon and FalconGuides are registered trademarks and Make Adventure Your Story is a trademark of The Rowman & Littlefield Publishing Group, Inc.

Distributed by NATIONAL BOOK NETWORK

All photos by Tom Hammell unless otherwise noted
Maps by Melissa Baker, The Rowman & Littlefield Publishing Group, Inc.

British Library Cataloguing-in-Publication Information available

Library of Congress Cataloging-in-Publication Data

Names: Hammell, Tom, author.
Title: Best bike rides Gettysburg / Tom Hammell.
Description: Guilford, Connecticut : FalconGuides, [2021] | Includes index.
  | Summary: "A guide for tourists and beginner cyclists who want to
  explore the Gettysburg battlefield and other points of interest around
  Gettysburg on bike"— Provided by publisher.
Identifiers: LCCN 2020049002 (print) | LCCN 2020049003 (ebook) | ISBN
  9781493052233 (paperback) | ISBN 9781493052240 (epub)
Subjects: LCSH: Bicycle touring—Pennsylvania—Gettysburg—Guidebooks. |
  Cycling—Pennsylvania—Gettysburg—Guidebooks. | Gettysburg
  (Pa.)—Guidebooks.
Classification: LCC GV1045.5.P42 G484 2021 (print) | LCC GV1045.5.P42
  (ebook) | DDC 917.48/4204—dc23
LC record available at https://lccn.loc.gov/2020049002
LC ebook record available at https://lccn.loc.gov/2020049003

∞™ The paper used in this publication meets the minimum requirements of American National Standard for Information Sciences—Permanence of Paper for Printed Library Materials, ANSI/NISO Z39.48-1992.

Contents

Mummasburg Rd

US 30

Buford Ave

Lincoln Ave

Harrisburg St

34

GETTYSBURG

8

Reynolds Ave

Middle St

Washington St

Baltimore St

E Confederate Ave

Fairfield Rd

116

3, 5

W Confederate Ave

Steinwehr Ave

2, 9

1, 7   Hunt   Ave

6

**GETTYSBURG
NATIONAL
MILITARY
PARK**

Hancock   Ave

Pumping Station
Rd

Wheatfield Rd

Red Rock Rd

**EISENHOWER
NATIONAL
HISTORIC
SITE**

4

Taneytown Rd

S Confederate Ave

Emmitsburg Rd

134

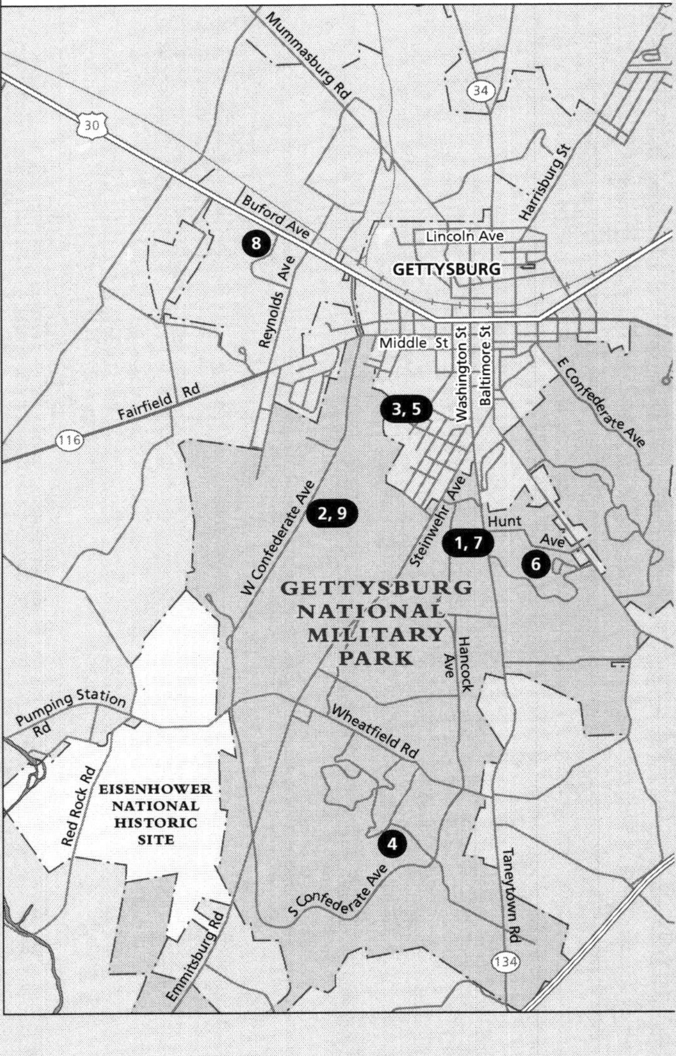

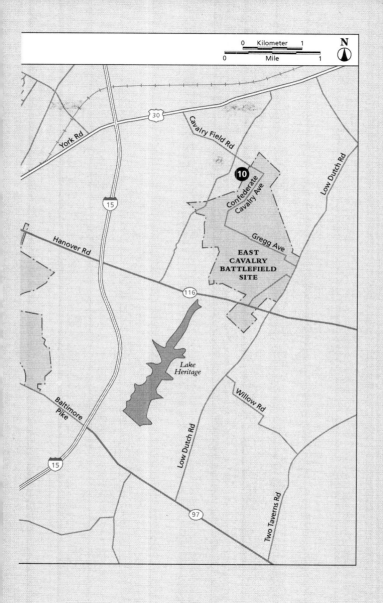

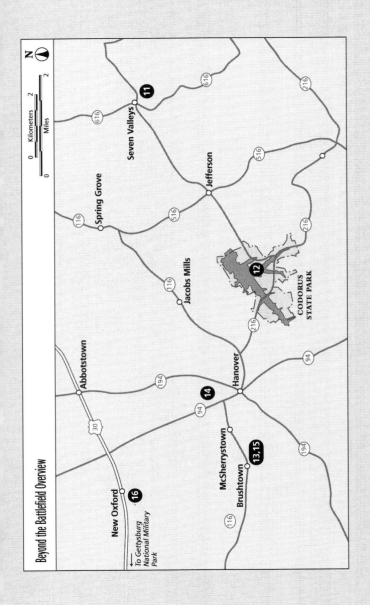

Beyond the Battlefield Overview

Acknowledgments

Creating a book like this is impossible without the help of many people along the way. I would first like to thank the people at Falcon for all the work they did to make the format and presentation of this book as clear and accurate as possible.

I also want to thank the Bicycle Club of Philadelphia (BCP) for introducing me to Gettysburg and the surrounding area and showing me the best places and roads to ride on.

I need to give a big thanks to Jim and his excellent wife Regina for coming out to Gettysburg and helping me work out the details for most of the rides in this book. The book is much better because of their input.

Lastly, I would like to thank my wife, Lorrie, who allows me the time to pursue my passion of biking and to take time away from her to work on this book.

Introduction

Gettysburg National Military Park is a national treasure and captures the history and emotions of an important moment of American history. The Battle of Gettysburg was the turning point of the Civil War and inspired Lincoln's famous Gettysburg Address.

Gettysburg is part of our national psyche and has been the subject of many books and documentaries, which is why Gettysburg National Military Park is a popular place to visit and gets over one million visitors a year. There are many ways to see and experience this national treasure, but one of the best ways to take it in and absorb it is by bike.

The purpose of this book is to show you the best ways to explore the Gettysburg battlefield and surrounding area by bike. Biking through the battlefield will allow you to cover the miles of roads at a relaxed pace and make it easy to stop anywhere along the way without worrying where to park the car.

There is a wealth of history to be explored in this park and hundreds of interesting monuments and statues to see. The variety and number of artifacts make it impossible to explore the park in full in a single day. That is why this book has divided the battlefield into a series of short rides so you can concentrate on different parts of the park depending on your interest and time.

This book will provide some historical context with each ride, but to fully understand the battle and the areas you will be riding through, you should check out some of the resources in the back of the book, as well as materials and programs offered in the visitor center.

The area around Gettysburg is one of the best and most beautiful places to go for a bike ride in Pennsylvania. That is why this book also has rides featuring some of the interesting sites in the nearby towns, including a restored Civil War train station, a pretzel factory, and a basilica. The rides are in the 4- to 20-mile range, allowing for a great afternoon outing or family adventure.

Even if you have visited this area before, exploring it by bike will give you a new appreciation of the historic significance and beauty to be found.

How to Use This Book

The rides in this book will allow you to explore the many different areas of the Gettysburg battlefield at your own pace and in your own way. The rides range from 4 to 20 miles, so it should be easy to find a ride to fit your needs. There are ten rides in and around the battlefield itself and six rides outside the battlefield, to the east of Gettysburg. The best way to choose a ride is to decide which area you want to explore and how long a ride you want to do. The overview map can give you a quick view of the rides and should help you decide which ones are best for you.

Most of the rides overlap other routes in this book. This was done intentionally to make it easier to string a couple rides together or create your own customized route by combining parts of different rides. If you have not visited Gettysburg before, it is recommended your first stop be the visitor center, where you can get a park map and talk to a park ranger who can help you get an overview of the battlefield.

All of the rides in this book are presented in a standard format that will give you the information you need about the ride so you will know exactly what to expect. The ride information includes:

Start: Starting location of the ride, including the address.

Distance: Total length of ride as well as ride type (loop or out and back).

Approximate riding time: This is based on the time a person in average shape would take to complete the ride and adds some time for the stops you may make along the way to view the monuments and scenic lookouts.

Best bike: Best bike for the terrain and ride surface—road, mountain, or hybrid.

Terrain and surface type: A general description of the road surface.

Highlights: A list of the main attractions or highlights along the way.

Hazards: This part describes any hazards that you need to watch out for during the ride, like traffic or tough intersections.

Other considerations: Anything extra you should know or consider before beginning the ride.

Maps: Each ride contains a simple map that shows the route and the major landmarks. (*Note:* The maps in the book are for general navigation only. I recommend bringing a park map with you, as it will have more details about the roads and sights on the battlefield and help you find a restroom or place to get water.)

Getting there: How to reach the starting location, including GPS coordinates. All of the directions begin from the middle of Gettysburg.

Each ride also has a few paragraphs describing the trip. The description highlights the major sights on the ride and points out any difficult turns, hazards, or terrain.

Every care has been taken to make the miles and directions as accurate as possible, but because you will probably go off-course or double back to see a monument, you will probably not ride the route exactly as it is laid out. Your riding time will also vary a lot depending on how often you stop to see the sights. That's okay—these rides are meant to be rides of discovery and scenic views as much as they are a form of exercise.

The area you will be riding in is neither flat nor extremely hilly. The terrain is mostly rolling hills, and most of the hills you encounter should not be a problem for anyone in moderate shape. However, there are some hills like the climbs up Little Round Top and Culp's Hill that may be a challenge to some. I try to call out any difficult terrain in the ride description so that you are aware of it ahead of time.

Because this area is filled with other people sightseeing in cars, on foot, or even horseback, the roads can be crowded and congested at times. That is why I recommend taking a few minutes to review the safety section of this book for some tips on how to avoid any problems while riding.

Safety

Bike riding, like any other sport, comes with its own set of problems and safety risks. These risks can be greatly reduced by following some simple rules and using common sense.

- **Be visible:** The most important safety rule is to always be visible. When riding a bike, you will be riding in and among cars, other bikes, and pedestrians, so it is important that they see you.

- **Signal your intentions:** Besides being visible, it's important that other people on the road know where you are going and when you are going to make a turn. This includes the usual hand signals for left and right turns as well as signaling for stopping and changing lanes.

- **Ride predictably:** When riding, especially in traffic, it is important to be predictable so other vehicles on the road know where you are going. Try to ride in a straight line in the same part of the road as much as possible.

- **Wear a helmet:** A helmet is the most important piece of safety gear to wear while riding. Riding a bike is very safe, but if you do take a fall, you have a much better chance of getting up and riding away if you have a helmet on.

- **Be careful:** The most dangerous thing on the road is not cars but other obstacles, like pedestrians, potholes, and other bikers. Make sure you always keep an eye on the path and obstacles ahead while looking around at the sights and scenery.

- **Maintain your bike:** Make sure your bike is in good working order, especially the condition of the brakes, tires, and gears. A properly working bike is safer and means less of a chance of your breaking down on the road.

- **Bring some friends along:** There is safety in numbers, so it is better to ride with a group if you can. It's also usually a lot more enjoyable to ride with some friends.

Map Legend

Transportation

═○15○═ Interstate/Divided Highway

═○30○═ US Highway

▬▬▬▬ Featured State, County, or Local Road

──○94○── State Highway

──── County/Local Road

■■■■■■■ Featured Bike Route

▪▪▪▪▪▪▪ Bike Route

- - - - - Trail

Land Use

⬚ National Battlefield Park

⬚ National Historic Site/State Park

Symbols

⌣ Bridge

▲ Campsite

🅿 Parking

🛆 Picnic Area

■ Point of Interest/Structure

🚻 Restrooms

○ Town

❶ Start of Ride

❷ Visitor Center

Hydrology

⬭ Lake/Reservoir

∿ River

Battlefield

The Gettysburg battlefield contains a treasure trove of information about the battle. There are more than 40 miles of road in the park that make it easy to explore the different parts of the battlefield on bike. The first ten rides will give you a number of different routes to get out and see any part of the battlefield that you are interested in.

1 Short Battlefield Loop

If you are looking for a short ride to give you a glimpse of some of the main areas of the battlefield, then try this one out. This ride takes you through some of the most popular parts of the Gettysburg battlefield and shows you some of the key monuments.

Start: Soldiers' National Cemetery parking lot, Cyclorama Drive
Distance: 4.1-mile loop
Approximate riding time: 1 hour
Best bike: Road or hybrid
Terrain and surface type: Park roads; mostly flat
Highlights: Cemetery Ridge, The Wheatfield, Pennsylvania Memorial
Hazards: You will be riding on park roads, so be careful while riding in traffic.
Other considerations: The streets and park roads can be crowded at times, so watch out for cars pulling out of parking spaces and people crossing the roads.
Maps: Google Maps
Getting there: Take US 30 (Lincoln Highway) to the center of Gettysburg. Make a left on S. Washington Street. Follow Washington Street south through town for just over a mile. The parking lot will be on the right, across from the cemetery. GPS: N39 49.02' / W77 14.16'

The Ride

This ride will take you along the main battle lines of the Union army and give you an overview of Cemetery Ridge and the wheat field where some of fiercest fighting of the battle occurred. To begin the ride, head out the back of the parking lot on Cyclorama Drive away from Route 134 (Taneytown Road), then make a quick left onto Hancock Avenue.

The Pennsylvania Memorial

As you head down Hancock Avenue, you are riding on Cemetery Hill, which is approximately where the Union line was on the last day of the battle. To your right is the field that the Confederate army had to cross during Pickett's charge. Be extra careful riding along here, as you are riding

GETTYSBURG CYCLORAMA

The Gettysburg Cyclorama is a large circular painting depicting the third day of the Gettysburg battle. It is 42 feet high and 377 feet long. Cycloramas were popular forms of entertainment in the late 1800s. The Gettysburg Cyclorama was originally housed in a building next to the parking lot where this ride starts, but was moved to the new Gettysburg National Military Park Museum and Visitor Center in 2008.

against the normal flow of traffic, and there can be a lot of people and cars on the road.

Bear left at the Pennsylvania Memorial. This is the largest monument on the battlefield and contains the full text of the historic Gettysburg Address. As you continue past the Pennsylvania Memorial, the road name will change to Sedgwick Avenue.

As you make the right onto Wheatfield Road, you are now riding through the area of the peach orchard and wheat field where some of the fiercest fighting occurred on the second day of the battle. The roads off to your left lead to the Devil's Den area, which is described in Ride 4.

There are not a lot of monuments on Sickles Avenue and United States Avenue, but you will see a couple farmhouses and may see some horses, as there are some trails for them along the road. Once you are back on Hancock Avenue, you will retrace your way back to the starting point. There are still many parts of the Gettysburg battlefield that you haven't seen, so if you have more time, you should check out the other rides.

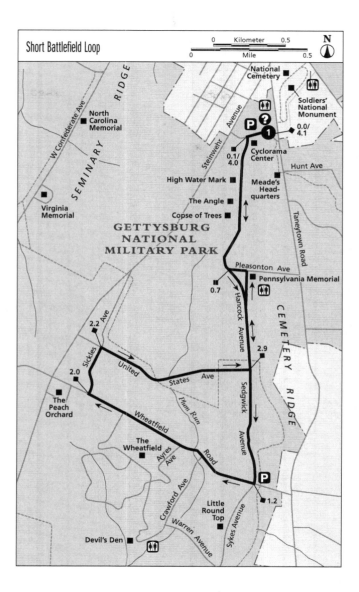

Short Battlefield Loop

Kilometer
0   0.5
Mile
0   0.5

N

National
Cemetery

Soldiers'
National
Monument

North
Carolina
Memorial

W Confederate Ave

RIDGE

SEMINARY

Steinwehr Avenue

P ?

1

0.0/
4.1

Cyclorama
Center

0.1/
4.0

Hunt Ave

High Water Mark

Meade's
Head-
quarters

Virginia
Memorial

The Angle

Copse of Trees

GETTYSBURG
NATIONAL
MILITARY PARK

Taneytown Road

Pleasonton Ave

0.7

Pennsylvania Memorial

Hancock Avenue

CEMETERY

2.2

Ave

Sickles

United

States   Ave

2.9

Sedgwick

RIDGE

2.0

The
Peach
Orchard

Plum Run

Wheatfield

Ayres Ave

Sedgwick

Avenue

The
Wheatfield

Road

P

Crawford Ave

Little
Round
Top

1.2

Warren   Avenue

Sykes Avenue

Devil's Den

Miles and Directions

0.0 Head out the back of the Soldiers' National Cemetery parking lot toward the battlefield.

0.1 Turn left onto Hancock Avenue.

0.7 Bear left at the Pennsylvania Memorial to stay on Hancock Avenue. Hancock Avenue will change names to Sedgwick Avenue after the intersection with United States Avenue.

1.2 Turn right on Wheatfield Road.

2.0 Turn right on Sickles Avenue.

2.2 Turn right on United States Avenue.

2.9 Turn left on Hancock Avenue.

4.0 Turn right on Cyclorama Drive.

4.1 Arrive back at the Soldiers' National Cemetery parking lot.

2 Essential Battlefield Loop

If you're looking for a ride to quickly see the main battlefield sites, then try this one. This ride will take you through the sites of most of the major battles and show you the more popular monuments.

Start: North Carolina Memorial on W. Confederate Avenue
Distance: 6.4-mile loop
Approximate riding time: 1-2 hours depending on stops
Best bike: Road or hybrid
Terrain and surface type: Paved city streets and park roads; mostly flat with a few rolling hills
Highlights: Seminary Ridge, Virginia Memorial, North Carolina Memorial, The Wheatfield, Pennsylvania Memorial
Hazards: You will be riding on city streets and park roads, so be careful while riding in traffic.
Other considerations: The streets and park roads can be crowded at times, so watch out for cars pulling out of parking spaces and people crossing the roads.
Maps: Google Maps
Getting there: Take US 30 (Lincoln Highway) to the center of Gettysburg. Go straight onto Spring Street when US 30 veers right onto Buford Avenue. Take Spring Street to Seminary Ridge and make a left turn on Seminary Ridge Avenue. After you go through the stoplight, the road changes to W. Confederate Avenue. The North Carolina Memorial is on the left in about a half mile. GPS: N39 49.08' / W77 14.88'

The Ride

This ride will give you a good quick overview of the parts of the battlefield and the variety of monuments to see. Begin your ride by continuing south on W. Confederate Avenue toward the Virginia Memorial.

Where you are riding now is Seminary Ridge, which was one of the main lines of battle for the Confederate army. You will notice some cannons to your left as you ride along and will get a good look at the field Pickett's men had to cross on the last day of battle. Farther down Confederate Avenue on the left you will see the large Virginia Memorial. This is a good place to stop and get a view of the battlefield looking toward the Union's positions on Cemetery Ridge. As you continue on Confederate Avenue, you will see more monuments to the Confederate states and outfits that fought here.

At the next main intersection you will make a left onto Millerstown Road. Be careful crossing Emmitsburg Road (US 15 Business). You are now riding through the area of the peach orchard and wheat field where some of the fiercest fighting occurred on the second day of the battle. To your right, in the distance, you will see the Big and Little Round Top hills, which can be explored in other routes in this book.

When you make the left onto Hancock Avenue, you will see the large Pennsylvania Memorial in the distance. This monument has an observation deck on top that can be accessed via a spiral staircase inside the monument. From here, you will continue along Cemetery Ridge, which was the Union's main battle line. You will then leave the park and make your way back to the starting point along some of the town's back streets.

THE SCALE OF THE FIGHTING

The second day's fighting involved at least 100,000 soldiers, of whom roughly 20,000 were killed, wounded, captured, or missing. The second day in itself ranks as the tenth-bloodiest battle of the Civil War.

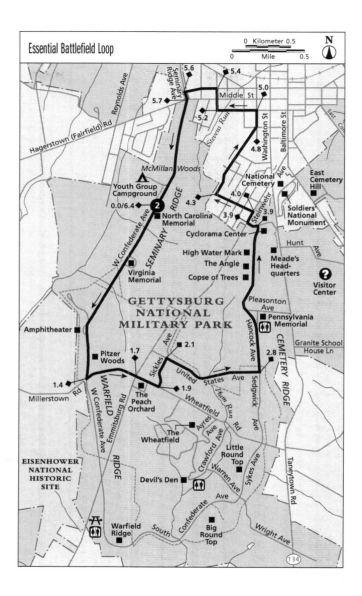

Essential Battlefield Loop

0 Kilometer 0.5
0 Mile 0.5

N

Reynolds Ave

Seminary Ridge Ave

5.6
5.4
5.0
5.7
Middle St
5.2
Washington St
Baltimore St
Hagerstown (Fairfield) Rd
Stevens Run
4.8

McMillan Woods
National Cemetery
East Cemetery Hill

Youth Group Campground
SEMINARY RIDGE
4.3
4.0
Steinwehr Ave
Soldiers National Monument

0.0/6.4
2
3.9
3.9

North Carolina Memorial
Cyclorama Center
Hunt Ave

High Water Mark
Meade's Head-quarters

The Angle
Visitor Center

Virginia Memorial
Copse of Trees

GETTYSBURG NATIONAL MILITARY PARK
Pleasonton Ave

W Confederate Ave
Hancock Ave

Amphitheater
Pennsylvania Memorial

Granite School House Ln

2.1
CEMETERY RIDGE

Pitzer Woods
1.7
Sickles Ave
United States Ave
2.8
Sedgwick Ave

1.4
1.9
Wheatfield Rd
7am Run

Millerstown Rd
WARFIELD RIDGE
The Peach Orchard
Ayres Ave

Emmitsburg Rd
The Wheatfield
Little Round Top
Sykes Ave

EISENHOWER NATIONAL HISTORIC SITE
Crawford Ave
Warren Ave
Taneytown Rd

Devil's Den

Warfield Ridge
South
Confederate Ave
Big Round Top
Wright Ave

134

Miles and Directions

0.0 From the North Carolina Memorial, head south on W. Confederate Avenue.

1.4 Turn left onto Millerstown Road.

1.7 Cross Emmitsburg Road (US 15 Business) and continue on Wheatfield Road.

1.9 Turn left onto Sickles Avenue.

2.1 Turn right onto United States Avenue.

2.8 Turn left onto Hancock Avenue.

3.1 Bear left at the Pennsylvania Memorial to stay on Hancock Avenue.

3.9 Turn left onto Cyclorama Drive, then make a right onto Steinwehr Avenue (US 15 Business).

4.0 Turn left onto King Street (by McDonald's).

4.3 Turn right onto Long Lane.

4.8 Turn right on Breckenridge Street, followed by an immediate left onto S. Franklin Street.

5.0 Turn left onto W. High Street.

5.2 Turn right onto S. Howard Avenue.

5.4 Turn left onto Springs Avenue, with a small climb ahead.

5.6 Turn left onto Seminary Ridge Avenue.

5.7 At the light, continue onto SW Confederate Avenue.

6.4 Arrive back at the North Carolina Memorial.

3 Full Battlefield Loop

For those who want to explore more of the battlefield, this ride will take you through all the major battle sites and past most of the popular monuments. This will give you a full overview of the three days of Gettysburg and an appreciation of how much there is to see in the park.

Start: Gettysburg Recreational Park, 545 Long Ln.
Distance: 10.4-mile loop
Approximate riding time: 1–2 hours depending on stops
Best bike: Road or hybrid
Terrain and surface type: Paved city streets and park roads; mostly flat with one climb up to the top of Little Round Top
Highlights: Seminary Ridge, Virginia Memorial, The Wheatfield, Little Round Top, Devil's Den, Pennsylvania Memorial
Hazards: You will be riding on city streets and park roads, so be careful while riding in traffic.

Other considerations: The streets and park roads can be crowded at times, so watch out for cars pulling out of parking spaces and people crossing the roads.
Maps: Google Maps
Getting there: Take US 30 (Lincoln Highway) to the center of Gettysburg. Make a left on S. Franklin Street. At Breckenridge Street, make a right followed by an immediate left turn onto Long Lane. Gettysburg Recreational Park will be ahead on your right. GPS: N39 49.44' / W77 14.34'

The Ride

Riding a bike around the different parts of the Gettysburg battlefield is the best way to appreciate the scale and magnitude of the battle. Begin your ride by making a left out of the park onto Long Lane. Watch out for traffic as you wind

A Civil War reenactor at Little Round Top

your way through town to get to Seminary Ridge. There is a small hill on Spring Avenue that you will have to climb.

Seminary Ridge Avenue will turn into Confederate Avenue. Seminary Ridge was one of the main lines of battle for the Confederate army. You will notice some cannons to your left as you ride along and get a good look at the field Pickett's men had to cross on the last day of battle.

Farther down Confederate Avenue on the left, you will see the large Virginia Memorial. This is a good place to stop and get a view of the battlefield looking toward the Union's positions on Cemetery Ridge. As you continue on Confederate Avenue, you will see more monuments to the Confederate states and outfits that fought here. Be careful crossing Emmitsburg Road (US 15 Business) as Confederate Avenue crosses it.

After you cross Emmitsburg Road, you will continue on Confederate Avenue and pass Big Round Top on your way to Little Round Top. There will be a gradual uphill until you cross Warren Avenue, then a steep short climb up to the top of Little Round Top. Be careful here, because there can be a lot of cars and pedestrian traffic. There is no better place to get a view of the entire battlefield, so I recommend that you get off your bike and walk to the top of the ridge.

The next part of the ride will take you through Devil's Den, the wheat field, and the peach orchard where some of the fiercest fighting occurred. You will then wind your way through the battlefield to Hancock Avenue and to the large Pennsylvania Memorial. This monument has an observation deck on top that can be accessed via a spiral staircase inside

BIKE RENTALS

If you don't want to bring your own bike to Gettysburg or don't have one, you can always rent a bike from **Getty's Bike Tours**. Conveniently located next to the visitor center, this company offers both bike rentals and bike tours. They rent adult and children's bicycles, and helmets are included with the rentals. They are located at 1195 Baltimore Pike, Gettysburg; (717) 752-7752; https://gettysbike.com.

the monument. From here, you will continue along Cemetery Ridge, which was the Union's main battle line, before making your way back to the starting point.

Miles and Directions

0.0 Turn left out of Gettysburg Recreational Park onto Long Lane.

0.2 Turn right on Breckenridge Street, followed by an immediate left onto S. Franklin Street.

0.4 Turn left onto W. High Street.

0.6 Turn right onto S. Howard Avenue.

0.8 Turn left onto Springs Avenue, with a small climb ahead.

1.0 Turn left onto Seminary Ridge Avenue.

1.1 At the light, continue onto SW Confederate Avenue.

4.0 Cross Emmitsburg Road (US 15 Business).

5.1 Dinosaur Bridge. This is where you can see some dinosaur footprints (see www.gettysburgdaily.com/gettysburg-dinosaur -footprints for details).

5.4 Pass a parking lot and portable toilets.

5.5 Cross Warren Avenue and continue onto Sykes Avenue. There is a short but steep climb ahead.

5.9 Turn left onto Wheatfield Road.

6.2 Turn left onto Crawford Avenue.

6.5 Crawford Avenue becomes Sickles Avenue.

7.5 Turn left onto Wheatfield Road.

7.6 Turn right onto Sickles Avenue.

7.8 Turn right onto United States Avenue.

8.5 Turn left onto Hancock Avenue.

8.9 Bear left at the Pennsylvania Memorial to stay on Hancock Avenue.

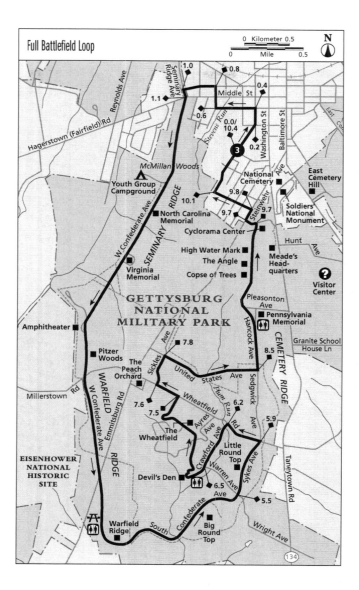

Full Battlefield Loop

0   Kilometer   0.5

0   Mile   0.5

N

Seminary Ridge Ave

1.0
0.8
Middle St
1.1
0.4
0.6
0.0/
10.4
0.2
Reynolds Ave
Hagerstown (Fairfield) Rd
Stevens Run
Washington St
Baltimore St

McMillan Woods
Youth Group
Campground
3
National Cemetery
East Cemetery Hill
9.8
10.1
SEMINARY RIDGE
9.7
9.7
Steinwehr
Soldiers National Monument
North Carolina Memorial
W Confederate Ave
Cyclorama Center
High Water Mark
The Angle
Copse of Trees
Hunt Ave
Meade's Head-quarters
Virginia Memorial

GETTYSBURG NATIONAL MILITARY PARK

Pleasonton Ave
Pennsylvania Memorial
Visitor Center
Amphitheater
Hancock Ave
Granite School House Ln
7.8
Pitzer Woods
Sickles Ave
United   States   Ave
8.5
CEMETERY RIDGE
Sedgwick Ave
The Peach Orchard
Wheatfield
WARFIELD RIDGE
Millerstown Rd
W Confederate Ave
Emmitsburg Rd
7.6
7.5
The Wheatfield
Ayres Ave
Plum Run
6.2
5.9
Crawford Ave
Little Round Top
Sykes Ave
Taneytown Rd
EISENHOWER NATIONAL HISTORIC SITE
Devil's Den
Warren Ave
6.5
5.5
Warfield Ridge
South   Confederate   Ave
Big Round Top
Wright Ave
134

9.7 Turn left onto Cyclorama Drive, then turn onto Steinwehr Avenue (US 15 Business).

9.8 Turn left after McDonald's (on the left) onto King Street.

10.1 Turn right onto Long Lane.

10.4 Turn left to arrive back at Gettysburg Recreational Park.

4 Devil's Den and the Wheatfield

This ride will take you on a tour of Little Round Top and Devil's Den. This is one of the more unique and interesting places in Gettysburg, so there is a lot to see on this short ride.

Start: Devil's Dens parking area, Sickles Avenue
Distance: 3.8-mile loop
Approximate riding time: 1 hour
Best bike: Road or hybrid
Terrain and surface type: Paved city streets and park roads; mostly flat with one climb up to the top of Little Round Top
Highlights: Little Round Top, Devil's Den, The Wheatfield
Hazards: You will be riding on city streets and park roads, so be careful while riding in traffic.
Other considerations: The streets and park roads can be crowded at times, so watch out for cars pulling out of parking spaces and people crossing the roads.
Maps: Google Maps
Getting there: Take US 30 (Lincoln Highway) to the center of Gettysburg. At the circle, go three-quarters around and head south on Baltimore Street. Make a right on Steinwehr Avenue (US 15 Business), then bear left on Taneytown Road (Route 134). Take a right onto Wheatfield Road, then a left at Crawford Avenue. The parking lot is on the left just after Warren Avenue. GPS: N39 43.14' / W77 14.40'

The Ride

Right across from where you parked is the boulder-strewn field that is Devil's Den. This and Little Round Top was the site of some of the fiercest fighting on July 2. To begin the ride, head back up Sickles Avenue toward Warren Avenue and make a right onto Warren.

The view from Little Round Top

The first half mile of the ride on Warren Avenue and Sykes will be an uphill grind. On Sykes Avenue you will have a steep, short climb up to the top of Little Round Top. Be careful here, because there can be a lot of cars and pedestrian traffic. There is no better place to get a view of the entire battlefield, so I recommend that you get off your bike and walk to the top of the ridge. This will also give you a great bird's-eye view of Devil's Den.

There is a lot to see on the top of Little Round Top, so take the time to take in all the monuments. When you're done, get back on your bike and head down the hill and make a left onto Wheatfield Road. You will then make the first left onto Crawford Avenue and ride back past the parking lot where you started. Those who don't want to climb the hill to Little Round Top can start the ride from this point for a shorter and easier ride.

As you continue on Sickles Avenue, you will wind through the boulders of Devil's Den before heading through the woods on Cross Avenue. Cross Avenue changes names to Brooke and then De Trobriand Avenue before the

WITNESS TREES

A witness tree is a tree that was alive during the Battle of Gettysburg. As of this writing, there are seventeen known witness trees. The oak tree on the left of Warren Avenue just after crossing the bridge from Sickles Avenue on this ride is the Devil's Den witness tree.

turn onto Sickles. There are not as many monuments in this part of the park, but the winding roads here are fun and easy to ride.

To your left when you make the right onto Wheatfield Road, the wheat field will be on your right, and the peach orchard will be to your left. This is where some of the main fighting took place on the first day of the battle. From here, you will follow Wheatfield Road back to Crawford Avenue to the parking lot where you started. If you have some time and energy left, you should take a walk among the boulders of Devil's Den for a closer look at this unique area.

Miles and Directions

0.0   Head north on Sickles Avenue from the Devil's Den parking lot.

0.1   Turn right onto Warren Avenue.

0.3   Turn left onto Sykes Avenue.

0.8   Turn left onto Wheatfield Road.

1.0   Turn left onto Crawford Avenue, which turns into Sickles Avenue.

1.8   Turn left onto Cross Avenue.

2.1   Road changes name to Brooke Avenue.

2.4   Road changes name to DeTrobriand Avenue.

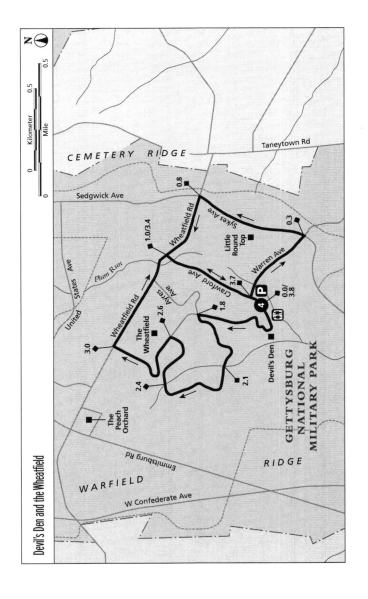

Devil's Den and the Wheatfield

GETTYSBURG NATIONAL MILITARY PARK

CEMETERY RIDGE

Taneytown Rd

Sedgwick Ave

Wheatfield Rd

0.8

Sykes Ave

0.3

Little Round Top

1.0/3.4

Plum Run

United States Ave

3.7

Crawford Ave

Warren Ave

Ayres Ave

Wheatfield Rd

3.0

The Wheatfield

2.6

2.4

1.8

2.1

0.0/3.8

4 P

Devil's Den

The Peach Orchard

Emmitsburg Rd

RIDGE

WARFIELD

W Confederate Ave

N

Kilometer

Mile

0   0.5

0   0.5

2.6 Turn left onto Sickles Avenue.

3.0 Turn right onto Wheatfield Road.

3.4 Turn right onto Crawford Avenue.

3.8 Arrive back at the Devil's Den parking lot.

5 Eternal Light Loop

The Eternal Light Peace Memorial is a symbol of peace dedicated on the seventy-fifth anniversary of the battle. It is a symbol of hope built to "guide us in unity and fellowship." This ride will take you on a loop to visit the Eternal Light Peace Memorial and show you some parts of the battlefield dedicated to events the occurred on the first day of the battle as well as the town of Gettysburg.

Start: Gettysburg Recreational Park, 545 Long Ln.
Distance: 5.8-mile loop
Approximate riding time: 1–2 hours depending on stops
Best bike: Road or hybrid
Terrain and surface type: Paved city streets and park roads; mostly flat with a few rolling hills
Highlights: McPherson Ridge, Eternal Light Peace Memorial, Gettysburg College, Gettysburg Train station
Hazards: You will be riding on city streets and park roads, so be careful while riding in traffic.

Other considerations: The streets and park roads can be crowded at times, so watch out for cars pulling out of parking spaces and people crossing the roads.
Maps: Google Maps
Getting there: Take US 30 (Lincoln Highway) to the center of Gettysburg. Make a left on S. Franklin Street. At Breckenridge Street, make a right followed by an immediate left turn onto Long Lane. Gettysburg Recreational Park will be ahead on your right. GPS: N39 49.44' / W77 14.34'

The Ride

The Gettysburg battlefield is filled with monuments, but probably one of the most important is the Eternal Light Peace Memorial dedicated to promoting peace. This ride will

The Eternal Light Peace Memorial

show you this monument as well as the area around it. Begin your ride by making a left out of the park onto Long Lane. Watch out for traffic as you wind your way through town to get to Seminary Ridge. Be careful when you make the left onto Chambersburg Road, as this is one of the main roads in the area.

Right before the left turn onto Stone-Meredith Avenue, there are two interesting monuments on the right. The first one is a man on a horse. This is John Fulton Reynolds, the highest-ranking officer killed in the battle. The other is a monument to Brigadier General John Buford Jr., whose cavalry division held the ridge here until the Union 1st Infantry arrived on the first day of the battle. One of the cannons at the base of the monument is the one that fired the first artillery shot of the Gettysburg battle.

On the right, right after you make the turn onto Stone-Meredith Avenue, is a small visitor center with a restroom. From here, you will make a loop around the monuments on McPherson's Ridge before crossing Chambersburg Road and making your way to the Eternal Light Peace Memorial.

ETERNAL FLAME?

The eternal flame you see today on the Eternal Light Peace Memorial has not been continuously burning since the dedication of the monument in 1938. The flame was replaced by a light-bulb in 1976 before being restored in 1988. The flame on this monument was the inspiration for the eternal flame on President Kennedy's grave.

The monument was dedicated by Franklin D. Roosevelt on July 3, 1938, on the seventy-fifth anniversary of the battle. The ceremony was attended by over 250,000 people, including around 1,800 veterans of the battle.

From the Eternal Light Peace Memorial, you will cross Mummasburg Road and pass an observation tower. Be careful not to miss the turn onto Robinson Avenue, as it is easy to miss. Once you are on Mummasburg Road, you will be heading into the town of Gettysburg and pass Gettysburg College. If you want to see the train station where Lincoln arrived to give the Gettysburg Address, you can take a left on Railroad Avenue to check it out.

Be careful as you make your way through town and back to the park where you started, as these streets can be a little busy at times.

Miles and Directions

0.0 Turn left out of Gettysburg Recreational Park onto Long Lane.

0.1 Turn right onto Breckenridge Street, followed by an immediate left onto S. Franklin Street.

0.4 Turn left onto W. High Street.

0.7 Turn right onto S. Howard Street.

0.8 Turn left onto Springs Avenue.

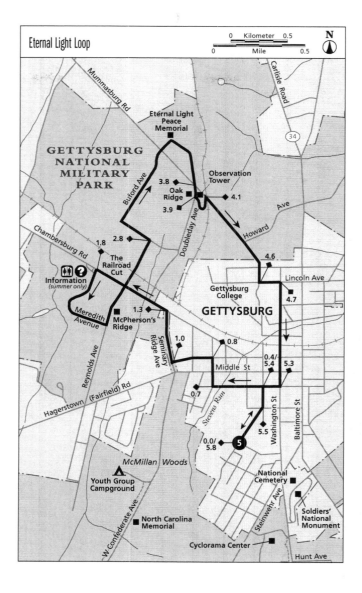

Eternal Light Loop

0   Kilometer   0.5

0   Mile   0.5

N

GETTYSBURG
NATIONAL
MILITARY
PARK

Mummasburg Rd

Carlisle Road

34

Eternal Light
Peace
Memorial

Buford Ave

Observation
Tower

3.8 ◆
Oak
Ridge   ◆ 4.1

3.9 ■

Doubleday Ave

Howard   Ave

Chambersburg Rd

1.8 ◆   2.8 ◆

The Railroad
Cut

♿🚻❓
Information
(summer only)

Meredith
Avenue

1.3 ◆
McPherson's
Ridge

Seminary
Ridge Ave

Reynolds Ave

4.6 ◆

Lincoln Ave

4.7 ◆

Gettysburg
College

GETTYSBURG

1.0 ◆

0.8 ◆

0.4/
5.4 ◆   5.3 ◆

Middle St

Hagerstown (Fairfield) Rd

0.7 ◆

Stevens Run

5.5 ◆

Washington St

Baltimore St

0.0/
5.8 ◆   ⑤

McMillan Woods

⛺
Youth Group
Campground

North Carolina
Memorial

W Confederate Ave

Steinwehr Ave

National
Cemetery ■

Soldiers'
National
Monument ■

Cyclorama Center ■

Hunt Ave

1.0	Turn right onto Seminary Ridge Avenue.
1.3	Turn left onto Chambersburg Road (US 30).
1.8	Turn left onto Stone-Meredith Avenue.
2.8	Turn left at the T onto Buford Avenue.
3.8	Cross Mummasburg Road onto Doubleday Avenue.
3.9	Make a quick left onto Robinson Avenue immediately after the observation tower.
4.1	Turn right onto Mummasburg Road.
4.6	Turn left onto W. Lincoln Avenue.
4.7	Turn right onto N. Washington Street.
5.3	Turn right onto W. High Street.
5.4	Turn left onto S. Franklin Street.
5.5	Turn right onto Breckenridge Street, followed by an immediate left onto Long Lane.
5.8	Turn left to arrive back at Gettysburg Recreational Park.

6 Culp's Hill

Culp's Hill was a critical defensive position for the Union army to protect their right flank. Although this is a less visited part of the battlefield, it is a fun place to ride and explore if you don't mind climbing a few hills.

Start: Gettysburg Visitor Center, 1195 Baltimore Pike
Distance: 5.6-mile loop
Approximate riding time: 1–2 hours depending on stops
Best bike: Road or hybrid
Terrain and surface type: Paved city streets and park roads; rolling hills with a couple steep climbs to get you up and over Culp's Hill
Highlights: Culp's Hill, Spangler's Spring, Gettysburg Visitor Center
Hazards: You will be riding on city roads and park roads, so be careful while riding in traffic.

Other considerations: The streets and park roads can be crowded at times, so watch out for cars pulling out of parking spaces and people crossing the roads.
Maps: Google Maps
Getting there: Take US 30 (Lincoln Highway) to the center of Gettysburg. At the circle go three-quarters around and head south on Baltimore Street. At the Y, stay on Baltimore Street by following Route 97. Follow signs to the visitor center, which will be on your right. GPS: N39 48.72' / W77 13.68'

The Ride

Culp's Hill was at the right of the Union fishhook, and although the battles fought there are not as well known, there is a lot of interesting history here. Begin your ride from the lot where you parked and head out toward Baltimore Pike. The mileage for this ride begins when you make the right onto Baltimore Pike.

Statue of Lincoln on a bench outside the visitor center

Baltimore Pike is a busy road, but there is a small shoulder on the right that you can safely ride in. Once you make the left onto Colgrove Avenue, you will be back on quieter park roads. The roads in and around Culp's Hill are beautiful and tree-covered. They are also a confusing set of one-way roads, so pay close attention to the map and directions.

As you wind your way up Colgrove Avenue and Carman Avenue, you will eventually come to Spangler's Spring. This small spring at the base of Culp's Hill was used by both sides during the battle. There are even stories of local truces called during the night of July 2 so that both sides could fill their

JOHN WESLEY CULP

John Wesley Culp was the nephew of Henry Culp, who was the owner of Culp's Hill. John fought for the Confederates in the 2nd Virginia Infantry. His regiment actually fought in Gettysburg on Culp's Hill. On July 3, John Wesley Culp was killed while carrying a message to a friend in town.

canteens. Today there is a small stone and concrete monument over the spring with a couple bronze plaques.

Right after you pass the spring, you will make a right onto Slocum Avenue and make your climb up to the top of Culp's Hill. Today, as it was during the battle, the summit of the hill is tree-covered, so there isn't much of a view. If you want a view, you will have to climb to the top of the observation tower, where you can see both the main battlefield and the East Cavalry field.

As you come down from Culp's Hill, you will keep bearing right at the next few intersections as you ride around some fields north of the hill. Eventually you will circle back to and through Spangler's Spring, but this time you will stay to the left and go up a more gradual climb that will get you back to Baltimore Pike and then back to the visitor center.

There is a lot to see in the visitor center, so if you have time, you should check out the museum, film, or especially the cyclorama.

Miles and Directions

0.0   From the visitor center, turn right onto Baltimore Pike.

0.2   Turn left onto Colgrove Avenue.

0.5   Turn right onto Carman Avenue.

0.7   Merge back onto Colgrove Avenue.

0.9   Turn right onto Slocum Avenue (immediately after the parking spots at Spangler's Spring).

1.1   At the Y, bear right to stay on Slocum Avenue.

1.4   Turn right onto Culp's Hill.

1.6   From the top of Culp's Hill, head back down the hill.

1.9   Turn right onto Wainwright Avenue.

2.3   Turn right onto Lefever Street.

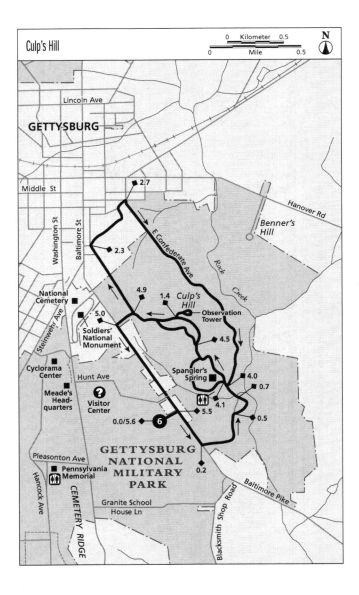

Culp's Hill

Kilometer 0.5
Mile 0.5

N

GETTYSBURG

Lincoln Ave

Middle St

Washington St

Baltimore St

National
Cemetery

5.0

4.9

Soldiers'
National
Monument

Steinwehr Ave

Cyclorama
Center

Meade's
Head-
quarters

Hunt Ave

Visitor
Center

0.0/5.6 ◆ 6

Hancock Ave

CEMETERY RIDGE

Pleasonton Ave

Pennsylvania
Memorial

Granite School
House Ln

2.7

2.3

E Confederate Ave

Hanover Rd

Benner's
Hill

Rock Creek

1.4 Culp's
Hill

Observation
Tower

4.5

Spangler's
Spring

4.0

0.7

4.1

5.5

0.5

0.2

GETTYSBURG
NATIONAL
MILITARY
PARK

Blacksmith Shop Road

Baltimore Pike

2.7	Make a sharp right onto E. Confederate Avenue.
4.0	Turn right onto Colgrove Avenue.
4.1	Turn left onto Geary Avenue.
4.4	Turn left at the T onto Slocum Avenue.
4.5	Bear left onto Williams Avenue.
4.9	Turn left onto Slocum Avenue.
5.0	Turn left onto Baltimore Pike.
5.6	Turn right to arrive back at the visitor center.

7 Town Tour

Gettysburg was the location of the largest battle of the Civil War and changed this town forever. While soldiers suffered on both sides, so did the civilians in town. This ride will take you through the town of Gettysburg and show you some of the many historic buildings.

Start: Soldiers' National Cemetery parking lot, Cyclorama Drive
Distance: 4.6-mile loop
Approximate riding time: 1–2 hours depending on stops
Best bike: Road or hybrid
Terrain and surface type: Mostly paved city streets; mostly flat with a couple small hills
Highlights: Lee's Headquarters, Jeanie Wade House, David Wills House, Gettysburg Lincoln Railroad Station, Shriver House, Soldiers' National Cemetery
Hazards: Most of this ride is on city streets, which means you will be riding in traffic and need to keep an eye out for traffic hazards as you enjoy the sights.
Other considerations: The streets and park roads can be crowded at times, so watch out for cars pulling out of parking spaces and people crossing the roads.
Maps: Google Maps
Getting there: Take US 30 (Lincoln Highway) to the center of Gettysburg. Make a left on S. Washington Street and follow it south through town for just over a mile. The parking lot will be on the right, across from the cemetery. GPS: N39 49.02' / W77 14.16'

The Ride

The town of Gettysburg was transformed by the battle here. Besides the many monuments on the battlefield, there are also many historic buildings in town. This ride will show you some of the main ones. It involves riding the streets of this

The Gettysburg Lincoln Railroad Station in the middle of town

town, which will have mild to heavy traffic, so you should not attempt this ride unless you are comfortable riding in traffic.

To begin the ride, make a left out of the parking lot onto Taneytown Road. On your right is the Soldiers' National Cemetery. No bikes are allowed in the cemetery, so if you want to tour it, you can do so on foot after the ride. This cemetery is the one that Lincoln dedicated as part of the Gettysburg Address, and the cemetery has a monument to that.

At the next intersection you will make a right onto Steinwehr Avenue (US 15 Business), then soon merge onto Baltimore Street. If you look to your right at the intersection of Steinwehr and Baltimore, you will see the Jennie Wade House on Baltimore Street. Jennie Wade was the only civilian casualty of the battle and was killed by a stray bullet.

WHY GETTYSBURG?

The town of Gettysburg had no strategic value, as it held no railroad or supply depots. It was, however, at the junction of a number of roads. Lee chose Gettysburg as a meeting point to gather his forces and then use the roads to march toward Harrisburg. It was only because of a chance meeting with Union forces in the area that the town became the location of the biggest battle of the Civil War.

As you continue up Baltimore Street, you will see a number of historic houses that were here during the battle. One of the more interesting ones is the Shriver House. This house was occupied by Confederate soldiers during the battle and is now a museum that shows how the civilians suffered during the battle.

A few blocks past the Shriver House, you will arrive at a circle at the top of Baltimore Street; be careful as you make your way around the circle. At the southeast corner of the circle is the David Wills House. This house was used as a hospital after the battle and was the house Lincoln stayed at and put the finishing touches on the Gettysburg Address.

After getting around the circle, you will see the Gettysburg Lincoln Railroad Station. This is the train station Lincoln arrived at and was also the station used to transport wounded soldiers out of the town. You will make a left here and ride next to the train tracks for a block before working your way to the western part of town and Lee's Headquarters.

The stone building on Chambersburg on top of Seminary Ridge was Lee's headquarters during the battle. There is a trail here, and there are some signs describing a number of different events that happened here. The house is now a museum but is only open on special occasions.

Once you are done looking over the property around the headquarters, you will retrace your way back to town and then go past the Gettysburg Recreational Park to get back to the parking lot where you started. Be careful making the left onto Steinwehr Avenue, as this road can be busy at times.

Miles and Directions

0.0   Turn left from the Soldiers' National Cemetery parking lot onto Taneytown Road.

0.3   Turn right onto Steinwehr Avenue (US 15 Business).

0.6   Turn left onto Baltimore Street (US 15 Business).

1.0   At the traffic circle, continue straight onto Carlisle Street (US 15 Business).

1.1   Turn left onto W. Railroad Street.

1.2   Turn left onto N. Washington Street.

1.4   Turn right onto W. Zerfing Alley.

1.6   Turn right onto West Street. Then turn left onto Springs Avenue.

2.0   Turn right onto Seminary Ridge Avenue.

2.3   Turn left onto Chambersburg Road, then turn right into Lee's Headquarters. After visiting the headquarters, turn left out of Lee's Headquarters, then make a quick right onto Seminary Ridge Avenue.

2.6   Turn left onto Springs Avenue.

2.8   Turn right onto S. Howard Avenue.

3.0   Turn left onto W. High Street.

3.2   Turn right onto West Street.

3.3   Turn left onto Breckenridge Street.

3.4   Turn right onto Long Lane.

3.9   Turn left onto King Street.

4.0   Turn right onto Sunset Avenue.

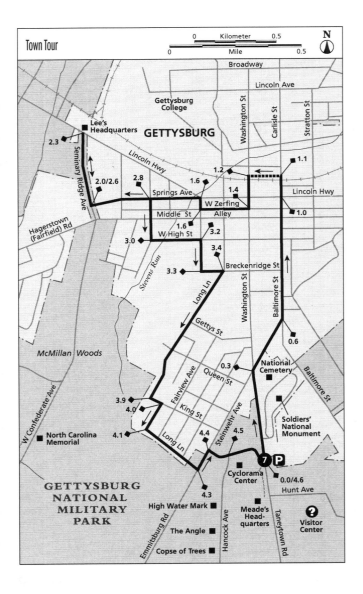

Town Tour

0 Kilometer 0.5

0 Mile 0.5

N

Broadway

Lincoln Ave

Washington St

Carlisle St

Stratton St

Gettysburg College

Lee's Headquarters

GETTYSBURG

2.3

Lincoln Hwy

Seminary Ridge Ave

2.0/2.6

2.8

Springs Ave

1.6

1.2

1.4

W Zerfing Alley

1.1

Lincoln Hwy

1.0

Hagerstown (Fairfield) Rd

Middle St

1.6

W High St

3.0

3.2

3.4

3.3

Breckenridge St

Stevens Run

Long Ln

Gettys St

Washington St

Baltimore St

0.6

McMillan Woods

Fairview Ave

Queen St

0.3

National Cemetery

Baltimore St

3.9

4.0

King St

4.1

North Carolina Memorial

W Confederate Ave

Long Ln

4.4

Steinwehr Ave

4.5

Soldiers' National Monument

GETTYSBURG NATIONAL MILITARY PARK

4.3

7 P

0.0/4.6

Cyclorama Center

Hunt Ave

Emmitsburg Rd

High Water Mark

Hancock Ave

Meade's Head-quarters

Taneytown Rd

?

Visitor Center

The Angle

Copse of Trees

4.1 Sunset Avenue turns left and becomes Long Lane.

4.3 Turn left onto Steinwehr Avenue.

4.4 Turn right onto Cyclorama Drive.

4.6 Arrive back at the parking lot where you started.

8 First Shot Ride

The first shot in the Battle of Gettysburg was fired 3 miles outside of town on Chambersburg Pike. There is a small monument marking the spot of the first shot, and if you are interested in seeing it, this ride will take you there.

Start: Gettysburg Information Booth, Chambersburg Pike (US 30)
Distance: 8.1 miles out and back
Approximate riding time: 1–1.5 hours
Best bike: Road or hybrid
Terrain and surface type: Paved roads; mostly flat with some rolling hills
Highlights: First Shot Monument
Hazards: This ride will mostly be on back roads, but there may be some traffic you will have to deal with.
Other considerations: The First Shot Monument is on a busy road, so you will have to be careful crossing that road to view it.
Maps: Google Maps
Getting there: Take US 30 (Lincoln Highway) through the town of Gettysburg and out the western side. The Gettysburg Information Booth will be on the left just after the light on Reynolds Avenue. GPS: N39 50.16' / W77 15.36'

The Ride

The Battle of Gettysburg started as a cavalry skirmish west of town and escalated into a much larger battle when the infantries met a little later. The first day's fight involved around 30,000 Confederate soldiers and 18,000 Union soldiers. This ride will take you along the path of the battle and bring you to the location of the first shot.

THE FIRST DAY'S BATTLE

The battle on the first day involved over 50,000 soldiers, with more than 16,000 killed, wounded, missing, or captured. If the Battle of Gettysburg ended after the first day, it would still rank in the top twenty bloodiest battles of the Civil War, with more casualties than Cold Harbor and almost as many as Fredericksburg.

To begin the ride, take Stone-Meredith Avenue, which is the park road to the left of the Gettysburg Information Booth. This will take you through some of the monuments on McPherson's Ridge. The monuments here honor the units from the Union and Confederate armies who fought each other on the first day of the battle.

You will leave the park when you make the right from Reynolds Avenue onto Hagerstown/Fairfield Road (Route 116) then make a quick right onto Old Mill Road. Old Mill is a back road, so although you may encounter some traffic, it should be light. The road has a bridge over Willoughby Run. Today this area is a residential neighborhood, but at the time of the battle it was wooded and some of the main conflicts between the infantries happened in this area.

You will be on this road for a little over 2 miles before making a right onto Knoxlyn Road. This road will take you to Chambersburg Road (US 30), directly across from the First Shot Monument. Chambersburg Road can be busy, so if you want to cross it to get closer to the monument, be careful.

The first shot of the battle was fired from this spot at a Confederate soldier at 7:30 a.m. on the morning of July 1 by Marcellus Jones of the 8th Illinois Cavalry. The monument is more a marker than a monument. It was placed here in 1886 with Jones and two other veterans present.

First Shot Ride

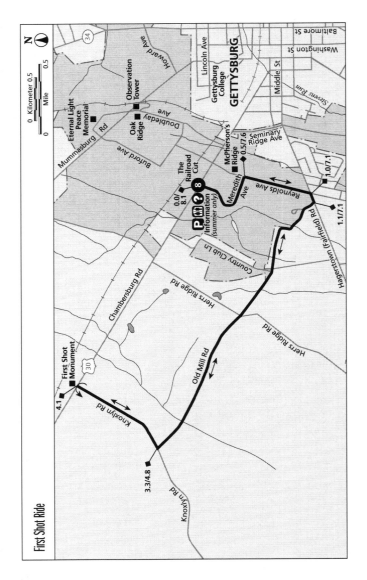

N

0 Kilometer 0.5
0   Mile   0.5

GETTYSBURG

Eternal Light
Peace
Memorial

Observation
Tower

Mummasburg Rd

Oak
Ridge

Buford Ave

Doubleday Ave

Howard Ave

Lincoln Ave

Gettysburg
College

Washington St

Middle St

Baltimore St

The
Railroad
Cut

0.0/
8.1

P 🚻 ❓ ⛽

Information
(summer only)

McPherson's
Ridge

0.5/7.6

Seminary
Ridge Ave

Meredith
Ave

Reynolds Ave

1.0/7.

1.1/7.1

Stevens Run

Hagerstown (Fairfield) Rd

Country Club Ln

Chambersburg Rd

Herrs Ridge Rd

Herrs Ridge Rd

Old Mill Rd

First Shot
Monument

4.1

30

Knoxlyn Rd

3.3/4.8

Knoxlyn Rd

34

Once you are done viewing the monument, you will retrace the roads back to the starting point. You will see a "Do Not Enter" sign when you turn onto Stone–Meredith Avenue, but this is meant for cars, not bikes. Just be on the lookout for any oncoming traffic.

Miles and Directions

0.0   Turn right from the Gettysburg Information Booth parking lot onto Stone-Meredith Avenue.

0.5   Turn right onto Reynolds Avenue.

1.0   Turn right onto Hagerstown/Fairfield Road (Route 116).

1.1   Turn right onto Old Mill Road.

3.3   Turn right onto Knoxlyn Road.

4.1   The First Shot Monument is just across Chambersburg Road (US 30). After visiting the monument turn around and head back down Knoxlyn Road.

4.8   Turn left onto Old Mill Road.

7.1   Turn left onto Route 116.

7.2   Turn left onto Reynolds Avenue S.

7.6   Turn left onto Stone-Meredith Avenue.

8.1   Arrive back at the Gettysburg Information Booth parking lot.

9 Sachs Covered Bridge

The Sachs Covered Bridge is a beautiful bridge with some interesting history tied to the Battle of Gettysburg. This ride will take you to the bridge and show you a couple interesting things along the way.

Start: North Carolina Memorial on SW Confederate Avenue
Distance: 8-mile loop
Approximate riding time: 1–2 hours depending on stops
Best bike: Road or hybrid
Terrain and surface type: Paved city streets and park roads; mostly flat with a few rolling hills
Highlights: North Carolina Memorial, Seminary Ridge, Virginia Memorial, Sachs Covered Bridge, John Eisenhower Bridge
Hazards: You will be riding on county and city roads as well as park roads, so be careful while riding in traffic.
Other considerations: The streets and park roads can be crowded at times, so watch out for cars pulling out of parking spaces and people crossing the roads.
Maps: Google Maps
Getting there: Take US 30 (Lincoln Highway) to the center of Gettysburg. Go straight onto Spring Street when US 30 veers right onto Buford Avenue. Take Spring Street to Seminary Ridge Avenue and make a left turn onto Seminary Ridge. After you go through the stoplight, the road changes to SW Confederate Avenue. The North Carolina Memorial is on the left in about a half mile. GPS: N39 49.08' / W77 14.88'

The Ride

This ride will take you out of the main battlefield and down to one of the main routes both Union and Confederate soldiers took to and from the Battle of Gettysburg. Begin your

Sachs Covered Bridge

ride by continuing south on SW Confederate Avenue toward the Virginia Memorial.

Where you are riding now is Seminary Ridge, which was one of the main lines of battle for the Confederate army. You will notice some cannons to your left as you ride along and will get a good look at the field Pickett's men had to cross on the last day of battle. Farther down Confederate Avenue on the left is the large Virginia Memorial. This is a good place to stop and get a view of the battlefield looking toward the Union's positions on Cemetery Ridge. As you continue on Confederate Avenue, you will see more monuments to the Confederate states and outfits that fought here.

At the next main intersection you will make a right onto Millerstown Road and leave the park. This will take you onto a couple of county roads, so keep an eye out for traffic. The next half mile on Millerstown Road will be a nice downhill glide until you make the left onto Red Rock Road. The next turn onto Waterworks Road will take you off the road across the John Eisenhower Bridge onto a pedestrian path. This bridge is named for the son of Dwight D. Eisenhower.

Waterworks Road will take you to the Sachs Covered Bridge. This bridge was built in 1854 and was used by a couple corps of Union troops to get to the battlefield. At the end of the battle, most of the Army of Northern Virginia retreated over this bridge. The bridge was damaged by a flood in June 1996 but was fully restored and rededicated in July 1997.

Cars are no longer allowed to ride over the Sachs Covered Bridge, but you can continue the route by riding your bike over it. You can get one last look at the covered bridge after you make the right onto Pumping Station Road and cross a bridge over the creek.

From here, you will go through some farmland and climb up a few hills as you make your way back to the starting point. The last part of the route has you riding a short stretch along Hagerstown/Fairfield Road (Route 116), which can have some traffic at times, so stay to the right in the shoulder until you get onto SW Confederate Avenue.

Miles and Directions

0.0 Head south from the North Carolina Memorial on SW Confederate Avenue.

1.3 Turn right onto Millerstown Road.

1.9 Turn left onto Red Rock Road.

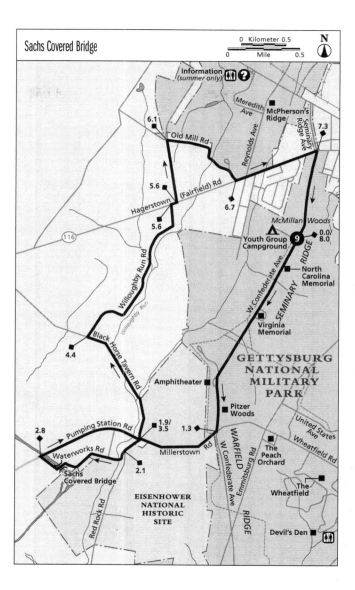

Sachs Covered Bridge

0   Kilometer   0.5

0   Mile   0.5

N

Information
(summer only)

Meredith Ave

McPherson's Ridge

Reynolds Ave

Seminary Ridge Ave

6.1

Old Mill Rd

7.3

5.6

(Fairfield) Rd

Hagerstown

6.7

McMillan Woods

5.6

Youth Group Campground

0.0/ 8.0

9

116

North Carolina Memorial

SEMINARY RIDGE

W Confederate Ave

Willoughby Run Rd

Virginia Memorial

Willoughby Run

4.4

Black Horse Tavern Rd

GETTYSBURG NATIONAL MILITARY PARK

Amphitheater

2.8

Pumping Station Rd

1.9/ 3.5

1.3

Pitzer Woods

United States Ave

Waterworks Rd

Millerstown Rd

W Confederate Ave

Emmitsburg Rd

The Peach Orchard

Wheatfield Rd

Sachs Covered Bridge

2.1

WARFIELD RIDGE

The Wheatfield

Red Rock Rd

EISENHOWER NATIONAL HISTORIC SITE

Devil's Den

2.1	Turn right onto Waterworks Road.
2.8	Turn right onto Pumping Station Road.
3.5	Turn left onto Black Horse Tavern Road.
4.4	Turn right onto Willoughby Run Road.
5.6	Turn right onto Hagerstown/Fairfield Road (Route 116), then make a quick left onto Park Avenue.
6.1	Turn right onto Old Mill Road.
6.7	Turn left onto Route 116.
7.3	Turn right onto SW Confederate Avenue.
8.0	Arrive back at the North Carolina Memorial.

10   East Cavalry Loop

Less than 1 percent of people visiting Gettysburg visit the East Cavalry field or know about the pivotal battle that was fought there. This ride will take you around the East Cavalry battlefield and explain some of the history.

Start: East Cavalry parking lot, Confederate Cavalry Avenue
Distance: 5.2-mile loop
Approximate riding time: 1–2 hours depending on stops
Best bike: Road or hybrid
Terrain and surface type: Paved county roads and park roads; mostly flat with a few rolling hills
Highlights: East Cavalry Field
Hazards: You will be riding on county and park roads, so be careful while riding in traffic.
Other considerations: The streets and park roads can be crowded at times, so watch out for cars pulling out of parking spaces and people crossing the roads.
Maps: Google Maps
Getting there: From Gettysburg, take Route 116 east toward Hanover. Make a left onto Low Dutch Road. Make the second left onto Gregg Avenue and follow it as it turns into Confederate Cavalry Avenue. There is a small parking lot on the left on Confederate Cavalry Road about 1.5 miles from the turn you made onto Gregg Avenue. GPS: N39 49.44' / W77 14.34'

The Ride

On July 3, the third day of the battle, a cavalry and artillery battle was fought in the area you will be riding. The Confederate army led by General J. E. B. Stuart was trying to attack the Union's flank. Stuart was opposed by General David Gregg. Although this was one of the smaller battles at Gettysburg, it was an important part of the Union's victory.

YOUNG GENERAL CUSTER

In June 1863, George Armstrong Custer was promoted to the rank of brigadier general at the age of twenty-three. During the East Cavalry field battle at Gettysburg, he famously became known as the "Boy General" when he repelled a pivotal Confederate assault led by J. E. B. Stuart.

To begin the ride, head south on Confederate Cavalry Avenue going back the way you drove in. You will notice some cannons and plaques from some of the Confederate artillery units that fought here. As you continue down the road, you will pass through some farm fields that are part of Rummel Farms. This area was the focus of an intense artillery and infantry battle.

You will see some more monuments and plaques to the different units that fought here. When the road makes a right turn, the name changes to Gregg Avenue. On your right a little ways down the road, you will see the largest monument in this area. It is to the Michigan 1st, 5th, 6th, and 7th Cavalries who fought here.

Gregg Avenue will come to a T, where you will make a right onto Low Dutch Road, then a quick right onto East Cavalry Avenue. You are now near the intersection of Low Dutch Road and Hanover Street, where General Gregg positioned his men on the morning of the battle to face the Confederate troops.

At the end of East Cavalry Avenue, you will have to make a right onto Hanover Street (Route 116). This can be a busy road, as it is the main east–west road in the area, so stay single file and in the small shoulder as you ride it.

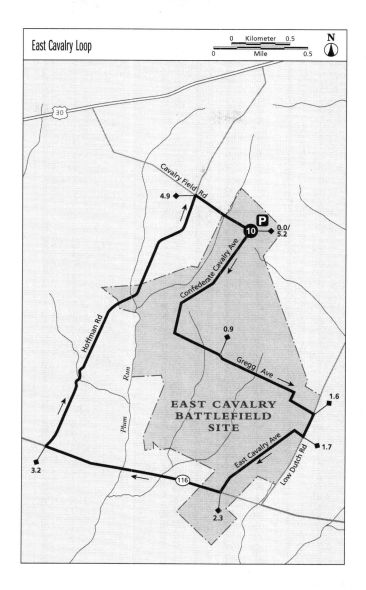

East Cavalry Loop

0   Kilometer   0.5
0   Mile   0.5

N

US 30

Cavalry Field Rd

4.9

P
10

0.0/
5.2

Confederate Cavalry Ave

Hoffman Rd

Plum Run

0.9

Gregg Ave

1.6

EAST CAVALRY
BATTLEFIELD
SITE

1.7

East Cavalry Ave

Low Dutch Rd

3.2

116

2.3

When you make the right onto Hoffman Road, you will see a small sign on the left corner describing some details of the battle, which will help you understand the events that happened here. Once on Hoffman Road, you will take it a little over a mile and a half through some quiet farmland before making a right on Cavalry Field Road, which will take you back to your starting point.

Miles and Directions

0.0 Head south from the East Cavalry parking lot on Confederate Cavalry Avenue (back the way you drove in).

0.9 The road becomes Gregg Avenue.

1.6 Turn right onto Low Dutch Road.

1.7 Turn right onto East Cavalry Avenue.

2.3 Turn right onto Route 116.

3.2 Turn right onto Hoffman Road.

4.9 Turn right onto Cavalry Field Road.

5.2 Arrive back at the East Cavalry parking lot.

Beyond the Battlefield

Riding through the Gettysburg battlefield can be fun and interesting, but there are a lot of good places to ride just outside of Gettysburg that you might want to explore. The next set of rides will show you some good places to ride that are fun and historically interesting, proving that the Gettysburg area has a lot to offer if you go beyond the battlefield.

11　Heritage Rail Trail

If you are looking to explore some rides outside of Gettysburg, the Heritage Rail Trail is one of the places you should check out. This 21-mile rail trail has some interesting sights to see and is a great place for a family ride.

Start: Hanover Junction Railroad Station, 2433 Seven Valleys Rd., Seven Valleys
Distance: 22 miles out and back if you head south, 20 miles out and back if you head north
Approximate riding time: 1–3 hours for each ride (north or south) depending on how far you go
Best bike: Mountain or hybrid
Terrain and surface type: Crushed stone rail trail
Highlights: Hanover Junction Railroad Station, Howard Tunnel, York, Mason-Dixon line
Hazards: You will be riding on a rail trail, which is free of any car traffic, but it is a multiuse trail so

you will have to be careful and yield to runners, walkers, and even horses.
Other considerations: There are limited places on the trail to get water and even less places to get food, so it is a good idea to bring enough food and water with you for the length of ride you plan to do.
Maps: Google Maps
Getting there: Take I-83 to exit 10 (Loganville) and North Street. Take Route 214 west to Route 616 south. The Hanover Junction Railroad Station is on the left about a mile after turning onto Route 616. GPS: N39 50.76' / W76 46.80'

The Ride

There are many different rides you can do on the Heritage Rail Trail. Although the starting point listed for this ride is the Hanover Junction Railroad Station, you can start the ride at any of the ten different parking lots along the trail. You can check out https://yorkcountypa.gov/images/pdf/Parks/2020_Heritage_Rail_Trail_Brochure.pdf for a map of the trail and directions to all of the parking areas.

The Heritage Rail Trail is a 10-foot-wide crushed stone path that goes from York, Pennsylvania, to the north all the way down to the Maryland state line/the Mason-Dixon line. The trail is reasonably level, but there are small elevation changes along the way. Facilities along the trail include picnic areas, drinking water, and restrooms. You will also be able to get food at some of the towns just off the trail.

This rail trail is unusual, because it is not a trail built where the train tracks used to be, but instead was built next to the train tracks. These tracks are still used, so please stay clear of them at all times. The train tracks are part of the old Northern Central Railroad and at the time of the Civil War were used to connect Washington, DC, with Harrisburg, Pennsylvania. Before the Battle of Gettysburg, the telegraph lines and some of the railroad bridges were targeted by Confederate troops to try to isolate Washington, DC, from other parts of the country.

This trail has a few interesting sites along its 21 miles. The main one is the 275-foot-long Howard Tunnel, which

STEAM RIDE INTO HISTORY

If you want to get the feel of what is was like to ride a train during the Civil War, you can take a ride on a steam train on the tracks along the Heritage Rail Trail. The train goes from New Freedom, Pennsylvania, to the Hanover Junction Railroad Station and not only provides a scenic ride but will also explain the history and importance of this railroad during the Civil War. For more details, check out their website, www.northerncentralrailway.com.

is about 5 miles north of the Hanover Junction Railroad Station. Besides the tunnel, there are a couple interesting railroad bridges and two historic train stations: the Hanover Junction station and the one at New Freedom. The train station at Hanover Junction served as a telegraph office and was a major source of transportation and communication between Gettysburg and Washington, DC. President Abraham Lincoln also changed trains here on his way to deliver the Gettysburg Address.

If you decide to head south from the Hanover Junction Railroad Station, you can actually make it all the way to Maryland and the Mason–Dixon line, which is about 11 miles away.

The miles and directions below contain the approximate distances to the different towns, parking areas, and sights from the Hanover Junction Railroad Station. This should help you decide which way to go and how far to ride. There are more restrooms and water stops going north. One of the more popular rides from the Hanover Junction station is to ride north to the town of York, stop in town for a bite to eat, and then head back. No matter which way you go, riding on the trail is a good way to spend a few hours.

Miles and Directions

North toward York

0.0   Start at the Hanover Junction Railroad Station.

2.0   Glatfelters Station (restroom).

4.5   Howard Tunnel.

5.2   Brillhart Station (water, restroom).

10.0   Town of York. Turn around and return the way you came.

20.0   Arrive back at the Hanover Junction Railroad Station.

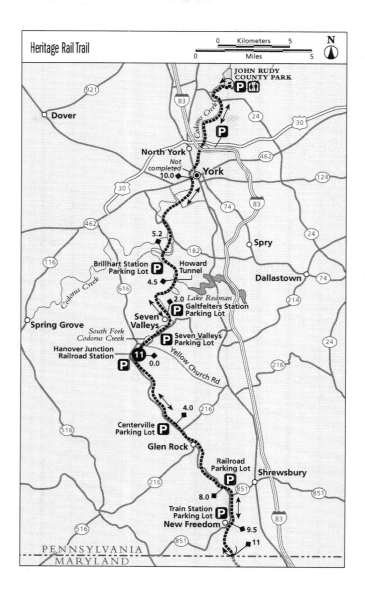

Heritage Rail Trail

| 0 | Kilometers | 5 |
| 0 | Miles | 5 |

N

JOHN RUDY
COUNTY PARK

P

921

83

Codorus Creek

24

30

Dover

North York

462

*Not
completed*
10.0

York

124

30

74

83

Spry

24

5.2

182

116

Brillhart Station
Parking Lot

P

Howard
Tunnel

4.5

Dallastown

74

616

2.0

Lake Redman

214

Codorus Creek

Galtfelters Station
Parking Lot

P

Spring Grove

*South Fork
Codorus Creek*

**Seven
Valleys**

Seven Valleys
Parking Lot

P

24

Hanover Junction
Railroad Station

P

11

0.0

Yellow Church Rd

216

516

4.0

216

Centerville
Parking Lot

P

Glen Rock

216

Railroad
Parking Lot

P

Shrewsbury

851

851

8.0

83

Train Station
Parking Lot

P

9.5

New Freedom

851

11

516

PENNSYLVANIA

MARYLAND

South toward New Freedom

0.0   Start at the Hanover Junction Railroad Station.

4.0   Centerville parking lot (no services).

8.0   Railroad parking lot (restroom).

9.5   New Freedom Railroad Station (water, restroom, museum).

11.0 Maryland state line / Mason-Dixon line. Turn around and return the way you came.

22.0 Arrive back at the Hanover Junction Railroad Station.

12 Codorus State Park

If you want to spend a day outside in nature, Codorus State Park is the place to go. This ride will take you around the park and show you its different areas and things to do.

Start: Main Boat Launch Area, Codorus State Park, Hanover
Distance: 9.4 miles out and back
Approximate riding time: 1 hour
Best bike: Road or hybrid
Terrain and surface type: Paved roads
Highlights: Lake Marburg, St. Paul's Union Church, Codorus Visitor Center
Hazards: You will be riding on county roads that may have some light traffic.
Other considerations: Be careful in the parking area, as it can be busy with cars, boats, and people at times.
Maps: Google Maps
Getting there: From the center of Gettysburg, take Route 116 east toward Hanover. Stay on Route 116 through McSherry-town and Hanover, then make a right onto Route 216 (Blooming Grove Road). After approximately 4 miles on Route 216, you will make a left onto Sinsheim Road. The road to the main boat launch area will be a half mile ahead on your left. GPS: N39 47.64' / W76 53.58'

The Ride

Codorus State Park is in York County, and its 3,500 acres sit around Lake Marburg. It is a popular place for picnicking, camping, and boating, both sailboats and motorboats. The lake is a rest stop for migrating birds and is a good place for doing some bird-watching.

This ride starts in the main boat launch area, a good place to get a nice view of the lake. To start the ride, head

LAKE MARBURG

Lake Marburg is a man-made lake, created by damming Codorus Creek in 1966. This was done to provide water for the town of Spring Grove and the water needed for the P. H. Glatfelter Company paper plant.

back out the park road and then make a right onto Sinsheim Road.

After you make the right onto Route 216 (Blooming Grove Road), you will go over a couple bridges and get some views of the lake. Route 216 may have some traffic at times, but there are wide shoulders to ride in to keep you away from the traffic. When you cross the second bridge, if you look to the right you will see the marina that you will visit next.

From Route 216 you will head down Marina Road all the way to the marina. (The road changes name to Marina Drive ²⁄₁₀ of a mile after the turn off of Route 216.) Besides the marina and some nice views of the lake, there is also a picnic area here as well as two disc golf courses.

As you continue the ride, you will head out the road you came in on back toward Route 216 and make the first right onto Marina Road. This will take you past a graveyard and to St. Paul's (Dubs) Union Church, where you will make a right and get back onto Route 216. Immediately after you make the right onto Smith Station Road, you will see a sign and driveway on the left to the Codorus Visitor Center. You can stop here if you want to get more information about the park or pick up a map.

As you continue down Smith Station Road, you will make your way along the lake to the sailboat launching ramp.

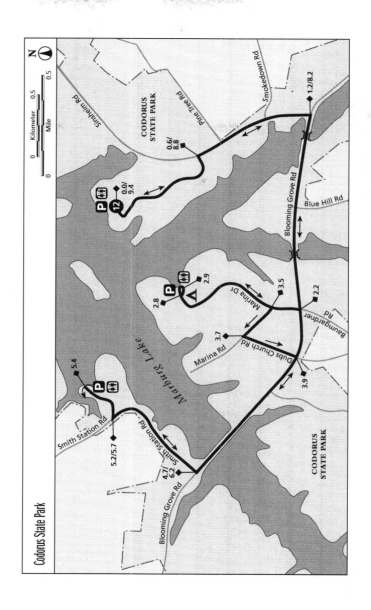

Codorus State Park

This is another good place to relax and enjoy the view of the lake. To finish the ride, you will make your way back out to Route 216 to return to the starting point.

Codorus State Park has a lot to offer, so after the ride you should check out the other activities available in the park.

Miles and Directions

0.0 Head away from the lake and boat launch area out the park road.

0.6 Turn right onto Sinsheim Road.

1.2 Turn right onto Route 216 (Blooming Grove Road).

2.2 Turn right onto Marina Road.

2.8 Turn right onto the park road to get to the marina.

2.9 Head back out the park road and make a left onto Marina Road.

3.5 Turn right onto Marina Road.

3.7 Turn left onto Dubs Church Road.

3.9 Turn right onto Route 216.

4.7 Turn right onto Smith Station Road.

5.2 Turn right onto unmarked road.

5.4 Reach the sailboat launch area, then turn around and head back out of the way you came in.

5.7 Turn left onto Smith Station Road.

6.2 Turn left onto Route 216.

8.2 Turn left onto Sinsheim Road.

8.8 Turn left onto the park road to get to the main boat launch area.

9.4 Arrive back at the main boat launch area.

13 Horse Farms

The country east of Gettysburg is filled with farms and quiet country roads. If you are looking for a scenic ride away from the battlefields, this is a good ride to try.

Start: Food Lion shopping center, 3744 Centennial Rd., Hanover
Distance: 11.4-mile loop
Approximate riding time: 1.5 hours
Best bike: Road or hybrid
Terrain and surface type: Paved roads
Highlights: Farmland, lots of farmland, and a few horses
Hazards: You will be riding on county roads that may have some light traffic and will occasionally cross a busy road.
Other considerations: Be on the lookout for the occasional farm implement crossing the road.
Maps: Google Maps
Getting there: From the center of Gettysburg, take Route 116 east toward Hanover for approximately 11 miles. Make a left onto Centennial Road and then a right into the Food Lion parking lot. GPS: N39 50.10' / W77 12.06'

The Ride

The area you will be traveling through on this ride will be mostly simple farmland, but if you look closely you will see some beautiful horses. This is because there are a couple of world-class horse breeders in the area, including Hanover Shoe Farms, which has bred some of the best harness-racing horses for the past seventy-five years.

To begin your ride, make a right out of the Food Lion parking lot onto Centennial Road. After you cross Route 116, you will be on Race Horse Road and then go through a residential neighborhood before riding through farmland

Riding by some of the horse farms in the area

and past some horse farms. Just south of where you are riding is Hanover Shoe Farms, so some of the horses you see as you pass by these farms may be the prized horses of harness racing.

After the horse farms, you will continue through some rolling hills and more farmland. There are very few trees and forest, so if it is a windy day, you will feel the full brunt of it. Eventually you will cross Route 116 again, but this time there won't be a light, so be careful, as there can be a lot of fast-moving traffic on that road.

BATTLE OF HANOVER
On June 30, 1863, before the Battle of Gettysburg, there was the Battle of Hanover. General J. E. B. Stuart slipped eastward across the path of the Union army and captured 125 wagons filled with supplies. Although this was a huge blow to the Union, it slowed Stuart's arrival at Gettysburg and was one of the many little things that contributed to the Confederates losing the Battle of Gettysburg.

Horse Farms

N

Kilometer   0   1
Mile   0   1

Oxford Ave
McSherrytown
Mount Pleasant Rd
Church St
Edgegrove
116
Food Lion
0.0/ 11.4
13
0.7
1.4
1.8
Race Horse Rd
Chapel Rd
Centennial Rd
Bender Rd
Brushtown
Hostetter Rd
Centennial
Hostetter Rd
Sells Station Rd
Hanover Rd
Howe Rd
3.2
8.8
Honda Rd
Hoffacker Rd
Littlestown Rd
4.3
Flatbush Rd
4.5
116
Storms Store Rd
Flatbush Rd
5.1
Square Corner
Storms Store Rd
Hoffacker Rd
School House Rd
6.3
Honda Rd
Whitehall Rd
Whitehall
5.8

Once you cross Route 116, you will stay on Honda Road and then make a right onto Centennial Road, which will bring you back to the Food Lion. There are a lot of quiet country roads out this way, so if you like this ride, feel free to explore other roads on your own.

A couple of the horse farms in this area offer tours and horse rides, so check them out if you are interested in finding out more about the horses in the area.

Miles and Directions

0.0   Turn right out of the Food Lion parking lot onto Centennial Road.

0.7   Turn left onto Sunday Drive.

1.4   Cross Route 116. The road becomes Race Horse Road.

1.8   The road name changes to Hostetter Road.

3.2   Turn left onto Hoover Road.

4.3   Turn right onto Sells Station Road.

4.5   Cross Littlestown Road. The road becomes Flatbush Road.

5.1   The road name changes to School House Road.

5.8   Turn right onto Honda Road.

7.5   Cross Route 116.

8.8   Turn right onto Centennial Road.

11.4   Arrive back at the Food Lion.

14 Pretzel Ride

Hanover is a snack food mecca, with four different snack food companies. It is a short drive from Gettysburg and a good place for a bike ride, especially if you want a snack afterward.

Start: YMCA parking lot, 500 George St., Hanover
Distance: 8.7-mile loop
Approximate riding time: 1 hour
Best bike: Road or hybrid
Terrain and surface type: Paved roads
Highlights: Utz factory outlet
Hazards: You will be riding on town and county roads that my have some light to moderate traffic and will occasionally cross a busy road.
Other considerations: Be careful not to eat more calories than you burn if you stop at the Utz factory outlet.
Maps: Google Maps
Getting there: From the center of Gettysburg, take Route 116 east toward Hanover for approximately 11 miles; the road will turn into Main Street and then Elm Street. A half mile after the road turns into Elm Street, make a left onto George Street. The YMCA parking lot will be about a half mile up on the left. GPS: N39 49.02' / W76 58.74'

The Ride

Hanover, Pennsylvania, is the center of the world when it comes to making pretzels. The companies of Utz, Snyder's of Hanover, Revonah Pretzels, and Wege of Hanover all make their home here. This ride will take you through some of the industrial sections of the town and then on some scenic roads north of town before stopping by the Utz factory outlet for a snack.

WHY HANOVER?

One of the main reasons pretzels were made and popularized in Hanover is because of the Pennsylvania Dutch. These German-speaking immigrants brought their old-world culinary knowledge to southeastern Pennsylvania and merged it with American innovation and industrialization. This led to tasty snacks that could be easily produced and distributed.

Begin the ride by exiting the YMCA parking lot onto George Road. Wilson Avenue is almost directly across from the parking lot, so take Wilson for four blocks and then make a left onto Moul Avenue.

You are now riding through the back end of town through a residential neighborhood. The next couple of turns will take you through some of the industrial sections of town. When you make the left onto Youngs Road, you will be leaving town and climbing a hill—about 150 feet in a mile. You will head through a tree-covered neighborhood before crossing Route 194 (Broadway) to get to Hershey Heights Road. Be careful crossing Route 194, as this road can be busy at times.

On Hershey Heights Road, you will have a scenic view of the valley and town below, along with a nice long downhill to enjoy. You will eventually come to a T where Flickinger Road meets Broadway. Across the way you will see one of the Utz factories. Here you will make a quick right onto Broadway, then a left at the light. You may encounter some heavy traffic here at times, so be cautious when making the left at the light.

From here, you will head back to the YMCA on the roads you came out on. When you get back to the YMCA, you will continue past it to get to the Utz factory outlet. The outlet is a mile from the YMCA parking lot via some residential streets. The Utz store isn't the only pretzel outlet in town, but it is one of the more popular ones in the area and always has a good variety of snacks.

After you have stocked up on some snacks, you can head back to the YMCA parking lot. But if you haven't had your fill of pretzels yet, you can check out some of the other pretzel outlets in town.

Miles and Directions

0.0   Head out of the YMCA parking lot across George Street onto Wilson Avenue.

0.3   Turn left onto Moul Avenue.

0.8   Turn right onto Fame Avenue.

1.2   Turn left onto Industrial Drive.

1.8   Turn left onto Gitts Run Road.

2.2   Turn right onto Moulstown Road.

2.3   Turn left onto Youngs Road.

3.7   Turn left onto Route 194 (Broadway).

3.8   Turn right onto Hershey Heights Road.

4.7   Turn left onto Flickinger Road.

5.7   Turn right onto Broadway.

5.8   Turn left onto Moulstown Road.

5.9   Turn right onto Moul Avenue.

6.5   Turn right onto Wilson Avenue.

6.8   Turn left onto George Street.

7.0   Turn right onto Grant Drive.

7.1   Turn left onto Clearview Road.

7.7   Arrive at the Utz factory outlet. After visiting the store, turn right onto Clearview Road from the Utz factory outlet.

Pretzel Ride

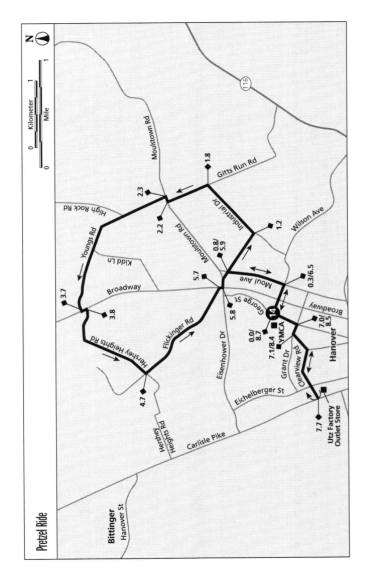

Bittinger

Hanover St

Carlisle Pike

Hershey Heights Rd

Hershey Heights Rd

Flickinger Rd

Eichelberger St

Eisenhower Dr

Broadway

Kidd Ln

Youngs Rd

High Rock Rd

Moulstown Rd

Gitts Run Rd

Industrial Dr

Wilson Ave

Moul Ave

Moulstown Rd

George St

Grant Dr

Clearview Rd

Broadway

Hanover

Utz Factory Outlet Store

YMCA

N

0   Kilometer   1

0   Mile   1

116

8.4 Turn right onto Grant Drive.

8.5 Turn left onto George Street.

8.7 Arrive back at the YMCA.

15 Edgegrove Basilica

The Edgegrove Basilica is oldest church in the area and has an interesting history. This ride will take you along some quiet country roads past the church so you can have a closer look.

Start: Food Lion shopping center, 3744 Centennial Rd., Hanover
Distance: 7-mile loop
Approximate riding time: 1 hour
Best bike: Road or hybrid
Terrain and surface type: Paved roads
Highlights: Sacred Heart (Edgegrove) Basilica
Hazards: You will be riding on town and county roads that may have some light to moderate traffic and will occasionally cross a busy road.

Other considerations: When riding around the basilica, please be respectful of any service or social activity going on.
Maps: Google Maps
Getting there: From the center of Gettysburg, take Route 116 east toward Hanover for approximately 11 miles. Make a left onto Centennial Road and then a right into the Food Lion parking lot. GPS: N39 50.10' / W77 12.11'

The Ride

The Sacred Heart Basilica, better known as the Edgegrove Basilica, is one of the oldest Catholic churches in America and was raised to a basilica by Pope John XXIII in 1962, which is a special honor for a church. The basilica is one of the most distinguished landmarks in the area and worth a visit.

To begin the ride, make a right out of the Food Lion parking lot onto Centennial Road away from Route 116. You will be riding through some farmland sprinkled with

Edgegrove Basilica in Hanover

residential areas. In just under 2 miles, you will make a right onto Irishtown Road. This road will take you past more farmland and through some forested areas. Keep an eye on the cue sheet, as you will have to make a couple of turns to stay on Irishtown Road.

At the end of Irishtown Road will be a short but annoying hill. After that you will make a right onto Black Lane. After about a mile on Black Lane, you should see the basilica on your right. You will then make a right turn onto Chapel Road, where you will have a clear view of the basilica, and then make a left into the driveway of the basilica and through the parking lot.

It's worth a stop here to get a closer look at the basilica, the area around it, and the surrounding buildings. Besides the church, there is also a school and a picnic area.

WHAT'S A BASILICA?

One of the great honors for a Catholic church is to be named a minor basilica, like the Edgegrove Basilica. To become a basilica a church has to petition for it and fulfill certain requirements. The church must be a large church that is well known and renowned for religious celebration. It must also stand out as a center of active and pastoral liturgy. It is not easy for a church to become a minor basilica, but if it achieves this honor, it signifies a link between the church and St. Peter's Basilica in Rome and the Supreme Pontiff.

After leaving the basilica grounds, you will make your way back through the outskirts of McSherrytown to the starting point at Food Lion.

Miles and Directions

0.0 Turn right out of the Food Lion parking lot onto Centennial Road (away from Route 116).

1.8 Turn right onto Irishtown Road.

2.5 Turn left at the T to stay on Irishtown Road.

2.6 Turn right to stay on Irishtown Road.

3.5 Turn right onto Black Lane.

4.5 Black Lane becomes Edgegrove Road.

4.6 Turn right onto Chapel Road.

4.7 Bear left onto Basilica Drive to go around the church.

5.0 Turn right onto Edgegrove Road.

5.2 Turn right onto Church Street.

6.1 Church Street becomes N. 2nd Street.

6.3 Turn right onto North Street.

Edgegrove Basilica

| 0 | Kilometer | 1 |
| 0 | Mile | 1 |

N

Irishtown Rd

Red Hill Rd

Dover St

Kohler Mill Rd

Mount Misery Rd

Irishtown

3.5

Irishtown Rd

Oxford Ave

Fish and Game Rd

2.6

2.5

Edgegrove Rd

4.5

Edgegrove

4.6

5.0

Peanut Dr

5.2

4.7

Edgegrove Basilica

Irishtown Rd

Centennial

Chapel Rd

1.8

Church St

Bender Rd

6.1

Centennial Rd

Oak Ln

6.3

Food Lion

6.6

North St

Main St

0.0/ 7.0

15

McSherrystown

Sunday Dr

6.7

Water St

116

Hanover Rd

6.9

Brushtown

6.6 North Street turns left and becomes Front Street.

6.7 Turn right onto Route 116 (Main Street).

6.9 Turn right onto Centennial Road.

7.0 Arrive back at the Food Lion parking lot.

16 Fish and Game

The area outside Gettysburg is filled with plenty of places for fishing and hunting. It is also a nice place to take a bike ride. This ride will take you through some of the quieter roads in the area.

Start: New Oxford town square, New Oxford
Distance: 9.5-mile loop
Approximate riding time: 1 hour
Best bike: Road or hybrid
Terrain and surface type: Paved roads
Highlights: New Oxford, Storm Stone Bridge, possibly an elephant
Hazards: You will be riding on town and county roads that may have some light to moderate traffic and will occasionally cross a busy road.

Other considerations: Be especially careful at the start of the ride by the circle, as this can be a high-traffic area at rush hour.
Maps: Google Maps
Getting there: From the center of Gettysburg, take US 30 (Lincoln Highway) east for 18 miles until you reach the circle that is the town square of New Oxford. Park in any parking space around the circle. GPS: N39 51.66' / W77 03.36'

The Ride

New Oxford is one of the best places in Pennsylvania to find antiques. That may be why this town has so many older buildings and seems stuck in the past. The town square where you parked is the center of town and may be a little busy, but once you get out of town there shouldn't be much traffic.

To begin your ride, exit the circle onto Hanover Street, which is on the south side of the circle and a quarter of the

The square in New Oxford

way around from where you entered from US 30. You will then make almost an immediate right onto W. High Street and head out the back of town.

It won't take you long to get out of town and onto quiet tree-covered roads. Most of these roads should only have occasional traffic. A lot of the roads you will be riding on will have tree cover that will give you some protection from the sun and wind.

At the left onto Storms Store Road, you will cross a beautiful old stone bridge. At the right onto Fish and Game Road you may hear a few gunshots, but don't be alarmed, as there is a shooting range nearby.

At 5.3 miles you will turn onto Irishtown Road, and at 6 miles there is a short climb to get to the next intersection, where you will make a left to stay on Irishtown Road.

When you are on Lingg Road, if you are lucky you may see an elephant (actually a statue of one) on the left side where the road curves. The statue is on the other side of the lake, so you have to look close to see it.

You are now almost back to town, and in a couple more turns you will be on US 30 (Lincoln Highway) and back at the circle where you started. On the northwest side of the circle is a coffee shop where you can get some coffee or something to eat and relax after the ride.

Miles and Directions

0.0 From the New Oxford town square, exit the circle onto Hanover Street (this is a quarter way around the circle from US 30 where you came in).

0.1 Turn right onto W. High Street.

0.5 Turn left onto Kohler Mill Road.

1.6 Turn right onto Fleshman Mill Road.

1.8 Turn left onto Kohler School Road.

2.1 Turn left to stay on Kohler School Road.

3.5 Turn left onto Stone Bridge Road.

4.1 Turn left onto Storms Store Road.

4.3 Turn right onto Fish and Game Road.

5.3 Turn left onto Irishtown Road.

6.2 Turn left to stay on Irishtown Road.

6.9 Turn right to stay on Irishtown Road.

7.6 Turn left onto Lingg Road.

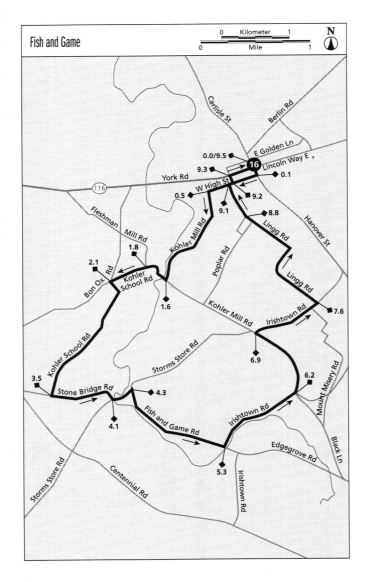

Fish and Game

0	Kilometer 1
0	Mile 1

N

8.8 Lingg Road becomes S. Water Street.

9.1 Turn right onto W. High Street.

9.2 Turn left onto Deihl Alley.

9.3 Turn right onto US 30 (Lincoln Highway).

9.5 Arrive back at the New Oxford town square.

Battlefield, Hotel, and Other Useful Links

Gettysburg and the surrounding counties have many things to see and do. Here are some links to help you find the best hotels, restaurants, and sights to see. I have also included some information about the local bike clubs and bike shops to help you find more rides that you can do in this area.

Battlefield Information

Your first stop when visiting Gettysburg National Military Park should be the National Park Service's website. This site provides detailed information about the battlefield park, including information on all the programs, events, and history of the park. There is even a section with tips on bicycling within the park.

www.nps.gov/gett/index.htm

If you want to get a quick overview of the battlefield, I recommend taking the virtual tour. This tour shows all the stops of the famous auto tour and gives you a good overview of the battlefield so you will have a better understanding of it when you do the rides.

www.nps.gov/gett/learn/photosmultimedia/virtualtour.htm

If you are interested in the history and details of the Gettysburg battle, I recommend the American Battlefield Trust site, which has detailed maps of each day's battles and some videos that will help you understand the various battles that occurred.

www.battlefields.org/learn/civil-war/battles/gettysburg

Hotel and Restaurant Information

Because Gettysburg is a major tourist attraction, there is an abundance of information about where to stay and where to eat. Besides the usual sites like Tripadvisor, I also recommend Destination Gettysburg (https://destinationgettysburg .com), as this site has a lot of good local information about hotels and restaurants as well as a full list of attractions in and around Gettysburg.

Bike Clubs and Bike Shops

Healthy Adams Bicycle/Pedestrian, Inc. (HABPI) is a nonprofit group of volunteers who work to develop walking and bicycling trails or paths in Adams County for recreation and transportation. Their main website (www.habpi .org/index.php) has a lot of information on riding the roads and trails around Gettysburg. They also have a page of maps and cue sheets (www.habpi.org/pages/onroad.php) listing a number of short and long rides in the area.

The Hanover Cyclers (www.hanovercyclers.org) was formed in 1974 and is the local bike club in the area. The club hosts a number of rides each week as well as a yearly Horse Farm Tour event.

Gettysburg Bicycle (https://gettysburgbicycle.com) is the local bike shop in town and offers bicycle sales, service, and rentals. They also have a list of road and mountain bike rides on their site.

Ride Index

About the Author

Tom Hammell has been riding a bike as long as he can remember. As an avid bike rider and member of the Princeton Freewheelers (PFW) and Bicycle Club of Philadelphia (BCP) he rides thousands of miles a year, leading other riders through the beautiful back roads of New Jersey and Pennsylvania, and spends at least a weekend a year riding around Gettysburg as part of the annual BCP Fall Foliage Trip. He has written two other books for FalconGuides, *Road Biking New Jersey* and *Best Bike Rides Philadelphia*. He lives in central New Jersey. You can follow his adventures on his blog at frisket.blogspot.com.